Leo Aylen
Sunflower
Poems

for Audrey
Thank you for
inviting me to
Queenswood

Leo Aylen

12 . 11 . 85

Sidgwick & Jackson
London

First published in Great Britain in 1976
by Sidgwick & Jackson Limited
Copyright © Leo Aylen 1976
2nd Impression 1979
3rd Impression 1982
4th Impression 1985

*

Poems from this book have been published in
Folk and Vision, Open the Door, Laugh or Cry or Yawn,
Tunes on a Tin Whistle, Sport and Leisure, Bridges,
The Poetry Makers, It makes you Think, and other anthologies
by Heinemann, Hart-Davis, Macmillan, Cassell, Longman,
Gleerups (Sweden), W.J. Thieme (Holland) and other publishers,
and broadcast by BBC, ATV, Thames TV, HTV,
and CBS (U.S.A.)

ISBN 0 283 98327 2 (soft cover)

Printed in Great Britain by
The Chameleon Press Limited, London SW18
for Sidgwick & Jackson Limited
1 Tavistock Chambers, Bloomsbury Way
London WC1A 2SG

Sunflower

Most of the poems in this book were written in America. Many of them even those not obviously American, could never have been written without the experience of America. I wanted to dedicate the book to an American friend or friends, but I discovered that I should have to make a list of a hundred names or more. And so the book is dedicated to all my American friends, and to all who have, knowingly or unknowingly, helped, encouraged or provoked me to write; not only poets and writers, singers, composers, actors, dancers and TV men; but also painters, designers, university professors, teachers, students, publishers, priests, photographers, politicians, doctors, social-workers, ad-men, architects, impresarios, agents, computer-technicians, health-food storekeepers, waiters, engineers, electricians and general handymen; not only in New York and its suburbs, but all over the country, from Seattle to Tallahassee, from the White Mountains of New Hampshire to the San Dia mountains of New Mexico, from a Vermont cop who decided not to book me for driving without a rear light when he was shown a book of my poems, to a Texas telephone engineer who swaggered in to repair phone-booths with his tools strapped in a low-slung cowboy revolver-holster. To all of them; to all my friends; my thanks, my love . . .

CONTENTS

SUNFLOWER AND VARIATIONS

Ah sunflower, weary of time,
Who countest the steps of the sun,
Seeking after that sweet golden clime
Where the traveller's journey is done:

Where the youth pined away with desire,
And the pale virgin shrouded in snow,
Arise from their graves and aspire
Where my sunflower wishes to go.

William Blake

I am hard at it, painting with the enthusiasm of a Marseillais eating bouillabaisse, which won't surprise you when you know that what I'm at is the painting of some great sunflowers.

Vincent Van Gogh

'Ah'

1.   **Syllable Poem**

Flow
Sun
Flow.
Low
Lower
Flow.

Lour
Sun
Lour.
Owl
Wolf
Lour.

Low
Lour
Woe.

Woe
Sun;
Woe
Flower;
Woe.

Owe.
Owe.
Owe
Woe.

Oh
Lone
Sunflower.
Oh.

'Sunflower'

2. Sunflower Leaves

Examine sunflower leaves
Through the glistening days of autumn.
At first, a fading: into the veins
Transparency seems to be pouring.

Later the leaves will shrivel,
Their pale green blacken.
Now the grey veins redden.
This death is a filling with blood.

'Weary of Time'

3. Van Gogh: Self-portrait with bandaged ear

This knife, this poison, this gun,
Turning my artist fingers to dung.
I fade. The colours halate.
The gun watches me paint.

My face grins from the sunflower disk
With an ear of torn petals, the blood neatly packed
Into paint-tubes, crates of sunflower seed,
Crates of fodder for postmen to eat.

'Who countest the steps of the sun'

4.   Cheyenne Sun-dance

Flat as biscuit the plains
Of a sun-baked, yellow-feathered tribe,
Who, sucked by their circle of dance
Like flies into flowers,

Raising their totem stalk,
On which are fixed
Skewers for ripping breast and back,
Gulp sun-power into their soul
By impaling their flesh on its pole.

'Seeking after'

5.   Old Maid with Birdseed

Old maid with hag's arthritic fingers
Crumbling dried flowers and bread-dust
To charm through your grubby lace curtains
Sparrow-chirps down on your seed-spattered
                                    cracked linoleum.

One cold evening in frost-pale autumn
A yellow flash of escaped canary
Swoops on your seeds, and, convict-on-the-run,
Scares the sparrows away from its song of
                                    sudden freedom.

'that sweet golden clime'

6. Sunflower Petals

Sunflower petals
Beginning to shrivel
Sculpt themselves
To metallic embracings,
Welded writhings,
Book of Kells
Traceries, Lindisfarne Gospels
Of twistings and wrigglings in gold.

'Where the traveller's journey is done'

7. La Berceuse (Madame Roulin, the Postman's wife)

Roulin
Red-bearded stranger, why d'you limp after whores
With your pale mad eyes screaming "Wait for me please"?
What more d'you need with a sun on your back
Like a long-service medal or a thick slice of cheese?

Van Gogh
That yellow cradle beside your bed . . .
Her apricot face and pumpkin breasts
Halating your parcels . . . Light's sunflower oil
Which pours from her seed-cake and well-darned vests.

'The traveller's journey is done
Where the youth pined away with desire'

8.   Vincent's Yellow House

With his hat full of candles for trapping the night
Vincent saw sunflowers hang in the sky,
Stuck them next day in an earthenware pot,
Painted them chunky as baskets and fruit.

Gauguin arrived at the butter house
And painted Vincent painting sunflowers.
Vincent of Gauguin's portrait said:
"It's certainly me, but me quite mad."

'And the pale virgin'

9.   The Business-man to the Air-hostess
on a Transatlantic Flight

Our time at this moment is five hours earlier,
Pale, pale girl of the neat white uniform.
Sunlight appears to be warming our windows
With the clouds fleecy rugs two miles beneath us.
Seat-belts unfastened, we stretch and relax
For your day-long minutes of lunchtime cocktail,
As we travel thousands of miles to Return-Ticket-Office,
Pale, pale girl of the neat white uniform.

Across the world we'll sleep tonight,
Pale, pale girl of the neat white uniform.
But all the rooms have identical beds.
Lady, untouched by love as any virgin,
Ninety-one men this year have filled you
With squirts of their sperm. Which face d'you remember,
Pale, pale girl of the neat white uniform,
Travelling thousands of miles to sleep in transit.

Lady, untouched by love as any virgin,
Travelling thousands of miles to sleep in transit,
Neither of us would dare
To arouse the other.
Can it be me tonight?

'Shrouded in snow'

10. North Face by Direct Ascent

"That was the way
He climbed: that crack
To where you see sunlight over those clouds."

Down on the ground
The spectators, tired of the crick in their necks,
Are about to relax,
Lower their telescopes and say,
"He must be dead. None of them will come back."

'Arise from their graves'

11. Self-portrait
*The more ugly, old, vicious, ill and poor I get, the more I want to
take my revenge by painting in brilliant colours, well-arrayed, resplendent.*
Vincent Van Gogh

Smile.
Your paint is poison,
Your sunlight . . . maggots of oily
Lead chromate, iron oxide.

Smile
As the maggots of poison
Crawl into your canvas eyes.
I smile for my oozing enemies.
The maggots impose my face
On emptiness.

'and aspire'

12. The Schizophrenic Stationmaster

They found him wearing his gold-braid hat,
Sitting cross-legged on the down platform,
Clutching his ticket-punch, stroking his cat,
Sipping tea from a tin mug hardly warm
And "Makin' a daisy-chain one mile long".

His wife ran off with a market-gardener,
Left for Westbury on the down train.
"Can I heat up your tea?" "Gives me heartburn."
He's had the shock treatment. Not a word of complaint.
He's "Makin' a daisy-chain one mile long."

'Where my sunflower'

13. There

Colours vibrating. Like seeing landscape in a flash of lightning.
Vincent Van Gogh

There, simply to be
Old boots, rush chair,
Sunflowers and earthenware,
Gnarled roots or olive tree,
But with the electrons visibly free
Is to be,
Simply,
There.

14. Crows over a Cornfield — the last picture

Well, my own work, - I am risking my life for it,
and my reason has half foundered owing to it.

Vincent Van Gogh

The lonely path leads to a field of wheat.
The black crow-cackle splits the royal-blue sky.
Twisting and flickering, the spinning heat
Upturns my sun-cracked head. Mirages. High
Over my eyes the spiky grain. I scratch. I crawl,
Scrabbling to clutch some moisture from the soil
And cool my sweat-caked face. Gasp, dazzled, fall.
Light like a whirlwind wipes me, and I boil.
No moisture ever - till that woman's tears.
Your tears, cream-breasted woman. You cradle fat
Gurgling weak babies. Cradle me - reborn.
Out of your womb I hack myself, slice ears,
Wrap them in parcels - bullets rip my hat.
My path has reached its point: these ears of corn.

APRICOT SADDLES

On apricot saddles we'll ride this summer,
Lassooing the sunshine with streamers of peaches,
Hats full of haycocks and walnut-patch britches
With moonshine-melon-and-seagull-swoop trimmings.

Who's for a sandcastle picnic with splodge?
Splodge in the mud, and splodge in the honey.
I'll treat you - the joy-stalls sell joy for a penny.
Let's joy-lick our joy-sticks and fly off the edge.

Let's spinnaker-whistle through summer's spray
Till we pull down the sunset stuck on to our kites.
Oh what monkey-tail-jumper and cat-pouncer nights.
What carousel-cantering-springboard days.

MOONLIGHT BONFIRE

Purple and silver the dancing whirls
Of satin and lamplight over the sand.
Flickering bonfire, twirling skirts
And old toad-woman, grinning and fat.

Spin through a summer of sunset-an'-moon
Accordion dancing to a head-drowse on shoulders
Rich as grease-licking fire-spitted food,
Sleepy with loving as route-marched soldiers.

Sink through the moonlight in an old elf-ballad
Sung to the embers by a thin nasal voice,
Till our dreams throng with minstrels and banners,
And magic blesses our girl, our boy.

RED-HEAD

Your hair is scraped carrots, but you're not for the sink.
You're more like to throw than to wash up a plate.
You're skimming and stone, water-boatman and pool,
Cream and a cat, suck and spit of a date,

Grip of deep roots and toss in the breeze.
With your dirty bare feet and your dress of leaf green
I shall crown you now with a hazel nut cap
Since you carry yourself as a hazel nut queen.

So beware of the squirrels in autumn my love.
Your dress has turned golden and red as your hair.
In pelting of apples and cracking of nuts
Your ripeness is ready, your brown limbs are bare.

"COME LIVE WITH ME AND BE MY LOVE"

The boy

If you'll give me a kiss and be my girl
Jump on my bike, we'll do a ton.
We'll explode from the city in a cloud of dust
And roar due west to the setting sun.

We'll bounce the days all over the beach,
Pop 'em like seaweed and scatter ourselves
Careless as kids with candy floss
Into all of the shapes of all of the shells.

We'll go as giddy as merry-go-rounds,
Bump with a crash like dodgem cars,
Float in a basket of coloured balloons
Or jump in a rocket and whizz for Mars.

If you love to be blown by a roar of wind,
If you love to twist and spin and twirl,
If you love to crash on the shore like waves,
Then give me a kiss and be my girl.

The girl

I love to be blown by a roar of wind,
But I love to watch the sea asleep
And breathe in salt and fresh-caught shrimps
As we wind our way through snoring streets.

I'll rave in a cellar till the band drops dead,
But I want you to sing on your own guitar
For no one but me and a moonlight oak,
Then dive in the silent lake for a star.

I love to spin the night away.
I love to hold you dark and still.
I love your kick that drives us miles.
I love the view from the top of a hill.

But if you give me the crashing waves
And sing me the blues of the sea as well,
Then, whether there's candy floss or not,
I'll give you a kiss and be your girl.

CHILD IN A SUNFLOWER FOREST

Snapping their thongs
Run,
Sudden as broken thong lash,
In bounding
Stumbling
Panic uphill.
Twenty bully-boys'
Burly tribal solemnity
Whip-lashed to roaring pursuit.
Blunderings
Up through tussocks and heather,
Ankles wrenching on outcrops and boulders.

Over the crest,
Sudden . .
Sheen . .
Of shimmering yellow . .
Sea? Shield? Sheet? . .
Acres of shifting, rippling, glistening, golden . . . ?
Centuries, seconds later,
In slither-race tripping and leaping downhill
Slide into a sunflower forest.
Stalks. Light like spinach.
Sapling stalks of ten-foot flowers.
Wriggle,
Vanish between them,
Not daring to tamper
With those serene vibrations
Of the distant, golden surface . . .

And so, escape . . . .

THE SEEDS OF LOVE

I've eaten a pile of seeds.
Roots have grown in me.
Vast golden sunflowers poke through my teeth,
Waggle backwards and forwards to reach the sun.
Pink blossom leaps out of my ears —
Must be the almonds.
That other pink-an'-white blossom
With knottier twigs,
Curling scratchily up round my armpits,
Is the start of my apple orchard —
Funny, I thought I spat out those pips.
My brain is growing corrugated;
It tastes as tangy as a walnut.
Well, when I'm a hundred years old,
Ridged and hard and grey,
You can saw me and plane me,
Cut me and dovetail me
Into a set of exquisite bedside tables.

But as for you,
I told you not to play with peach-stones.
Now you've grown so strokable
I shall have to peel off your skin,
Suck into you noisily
And gorge myself on your unbelievable golden juices.

TWENTY-FOUR HOUR LOVE AFFAIR
BETWEEN A SOLDIER AND A SICK GIRL IN WARTIME

i

Sick phosphorescence. Chlorinated air.
Bleaching green light.
Boots clanging down the bottomless stairs.

The iron sky splits,
A million welders hammering thunder sheets.

I touch your throat,
Your pain.
Behind us soldier corpses lie
Grey. Grey-green.

The war
Is everywhere
But here.

ii

The tower sways.
Steel bars disintegrate
To green-white shafts of fluorescent light.
Five hundred feet of marble shakes
Out in a blush-pale streak —
A tangent into space
Rushing with solar wind.
We stand
Within
The vortex, still.

Round us, the marble,
Flaking,
Displacing
Itself, cascading
In pink-white petals . . .

iii

Swimming through light
Slow-motion, weightless
Walking in underwater space,
Your throat my breathing tube.

Onlookers hurry past
Outside the glass,
Irrelevant.

Here, all our speed's the drift
Down with a stream's
Translucencies.
Safe as a light-dabbled pool . .
        that is bottomless . . absolute.

Do not dive deeper.
Ears will explode with the pressure.

Blood will flow.

iv

Fingertips brushing skin
Transparent as coral fish.

So thin
The spinal cord,
The link.

Fragile fingers
Caressing vertebrae,
Caressing the tiny bone-boxes stacked
For transmitting sensation,
Tapping out messages,
Signalling pain.

Electronic messages flash
In dots and dashes —
Prestissimo tapping.

Messages code into touch.

Morse-fingered caresses.

v

The peopled city sinks.
Those blocks and towers
Nothing but network of lights
Subsiding beneath a flight over oceans.
Millions of workers turn to ghosts now.

That one past moment continues real
Through a present of pain
Acetylene-slicing towers with pallid light
Flaking in showers of petals.

Some present!

Tear the wrappings
Ghosts cannot undo.

vi

One of us two has died already
At some point in the future.
The other is groping to be born.

White-coated men pass through our bodies
Which flow together again like water.

What century, what town?
What clicking heels
Trundling what bright steel trolleys
Into which morgue?
Whose love is sliding down
On silent, dark grey, rubber wheels?

For in what year
Was such a field
Of pink-white cherry-froth ever real?

vii

There cannot but be pain
Raining soot and smog, staining,
Crumpling and pushing down the petals
Into boot-pock-marked mud.
There cannot but be pain.

There cannot but be pain
Caning the lips apart, constraining,
Cramping the pounding heart.
Life-pump-blocked petals drop.
Bloodless limbs lock.
There cannot but be pain.

But are we ghosts now
Whose pain is over?

SATURDAY-NIGHT PICK-UP
for Bill and Ginnie

No, there's nothing more to say.
'Cause Billy's a tongue-tied orphan groping for words.
Groping for words like a spanner dropped down behind the boiler,
Groping for words in a criss-cross of greasy pipe-bends,
Groping for dusty words, grimed to his finger-nails.

And Betty has nothing to say,
Groping for words down dusty corridors,
Orphan-school corridors where books carried the cane.

Down dusty orphan-school corridors,
Where "Learn-a-pome" was next worst punishment after the strap,
Billy and Betty have nothing to say,
'Cause language was locked out of their reach in museums,
Labelled "For use by Ladies and Gentlemen only".

Billy and Betty have nothing to say,
Groping for words in a two-room flat,
Where making love - as opposed to having sex -
Was making sure that the steak was tender,
Scouring the frying-pan to make it shine.
Betty has nothing to say.

And Billy will never see
That putting a knob of butter on tender steaks is making love,
Getting grease up your fingernails for a shiny frying-pan is making love.

And Betty will never see
That getting grease up your fingernails and finding the spanner is making love,
Grease up your fingernails and the bearing mended is making love.

And neither will ever be able to say:
We're not the sort for Happy-ever-afters.
But, just for a moment, one Saturday night in Liverpool,
Our love, which is grease grimed into our finger-nails,
Engine grease, and grease from a frying-pan,
This love-grease mixed,
Mixed for a moment. caught fire,
Flamed in the cup of our hands
As bright as the love marked "Ladies and Gentlemen only".

I CANNOT ENTER

I cannot enter your surgical dreams,
Grab, and stop the knife
From slitting your nightmared body apart,
Only switch on a light,
Throw logs into this hearth,
Bake you some bread, some bacon and beans,
Pass you a bowl of well-thickened soup,
Then leave you to wait in your log-warmed room,
And walk out into my own dream-roughened night.

BY THE LIGHT OF ONE CANDLE

By the light of one candle
That is a pool of green liquid
Encasing a golden star,

The darkness of your body
Swallows me up in a forest
Filled with tail-feathered brilliance
Dazzling as Bird-of-Paradise.

Your inmost spaces
Translucent with golden fish
And opalescent sea-horses,
Liquefy my eyes,

Till the golden star
In the scented pool
Turns to a firmament flooded with Milky Ways.

DARKNESS OF BRANCHES AND CREEPERS

Darkness of branches and creepers.
Hot scent of moisture and lilies.
Your body-wrestlings
Flash scarlet, mauve, viridian humming-birds
                       up from the sweat-droplets.

We are encased
In glittering colour vibrations.
Heat pounds us
Down tunnels of ebony
Splintered by searchlight beams.

At last, washed through,
We emerge to float on water-lilies.
Alligators, tamed and harmless,
Frolic themselves into baby sea-lions,
Offer their backs to us, black, slide-shiny,
Carry us sleepily through the slippery
                       warm green lemon-scented water.

WHEN LOVERS TOUCH

Vilanelle

Our bodies burn, dissolve into a shoal,
Into a million fishes, jerked through a fire
Of rippling shimmers from your exploding soul.

Flame-demons swoop. Each claw's a lighted coal
To feed these flashes given off by the pyre
Our bodies burn. Dissolve into a shoal

Of salamanders, as in your caves a troll
Discovers diamonds, builds a giant spire
Of rippling shimmers from your exploding soul,

Until the diamond spire blossoms, a bowl
Of light-ray boomerangs. As wire meets wire,
Our bodies burn, dissolve into a shoal

Of fountain-drops. Each drop grows into a foal
Racing through meadows, quartering our shire
Of rippling shimmers. From your exploding soul

Stretch immense galaxies. There we float, whole,
But spread through a billion particles of desire.
Our bodies burn, dissolve into a shoal
Of rippling shimmers from your exploding soul.

SPOILT FRUIT

Vilanelle

Spoilt fruit, too quickly ripened, going bad —
Women with blotched complexions, grabbing drinks.
Lonely and lost, disorientated, mad,

We, envied rich, gather, discuss a fad
Over the olives. No one stops, and thinks:
"Spoilt fruit, too quickly ripened, going bad,"

Of that drunk matron's massive bosom clad
In teenage tightness. We flash our cuff-links.
Lonely and lost, disorientated, mad,

We can see nothing, and we cannot add
Up our experience. All's for kicks and kinks.
Spoilt fruit, too quickly ripened, going bad

And quickly chucked in trash-cans. We are glad
To greet the new, but age or failure stinks.
Lonely and lost, disorientated, mad,

We are the bright ones, blind; however sad
We may be, our tame mirror smirks and prinks:
Spoilt fruit, too quickly ripened, going bad,
Lonely and lost, disorientated, mad.

THE ABORTION AND THE ATTEMPTED SUICIDE

i

Naked I lie,
Sprawled on a marriage-bed
Brass-posted, wide as the sea.
Oozing from mirrors on the walls, caparisoned
Shadows loll over and finger me.

But never a man.

Only a shadow, spilling its oily flame,
That singed the hairs of my womb.
Only a streak of bleary
Scum smeared over my eyes,
Only the smudgy print of a grease-grimed thumb.

Never a man.

So pump the water, dissolve the oil,
Douse the flame — thin, silver knives
Slitting the threads of the shadow — watch them burn,
And smoke fizzle into the ground.
Bury with earth the stains and scum.

ii

Naked I lie,
Sprawled on a marriage-bed
Brass-posted, wide as the sea.
Flickering from mirrors on the wall, caparisoned
Silvery knives are fingering me,
Mincing in satin ribbons over my wrist,
Swelling inside me like viscous pills,
Balloons of marsh-gas, straining to lift
That grease-clogged body, spluttering to light
Gobbets of sulphurous flame
To glue together those rucks and tatters,
That stretched and twisted womb . .
Till the jagged edges . .
Blackly
Coagulate . . .

Ooze pitch . . .

Petrify . . . .

Lump
Junked.

POOR OLD JONES

Poor old Jones
Knobbles on his bones
Patches on his elbows and his pocket full of groans.

Chocolate cream
Sucked plumply
By sauntering sweet thirteen
Long since fucked into satisfied
Womanhood's regular orgasms
Of sexual All-Bran.
So succulent and easy.

Succulent and easy —
French, that language honed
Into Academician purity
By the precision-work phrases
Of Racine and Corneille,
Now squeezed from a tape-machine
Like Ultrabrite toothpaste
For cleaning yourself a smile
To seduce a Paris-Match pin-up
In a fortnight's school-sponsored Brittany holiday.
Succulent and easy.

Chocolate and cream!
Cracked cream plaster,
Blistering chocolate banisters,
Where we marched two and two
To jabber our jingles
Of multiplication tables,
Irregular verbs and esker-vous.
Not succulent. Not easy.
No Welfare State
To pay our fares,
No holidays in French hotels
With subsistence allowance,
Education Board cameras
And free contraceptive pills
Coated in rose-pink sugar,
Succulently easy.

This hall —
Landscapes and poetry paper the wall.
This smell —
No stale boiled cabbage
Eighty-five centuries old —
Crisp, buttery baking;
Forty plump, white-capped teenagers'
Home-made apple tart.
This sound
Of the Royal Phil
In perfect amplified stereo
Mounting us with Sacre de Printemps'
Tantrums of bliss,
Its fertile succulence.
And so . . . easy.

Succulent and easy,
That writhing, running and waving of arms,
Heaving of breasts,
Wriggling of arses
Into Stravinsky's phallic ecstasy.
The gym floor
Melts with the heat of the tight-red-pants drama class,
While young Mr. Right Wright
In his white polo-neck and turquoise levis
Is apparently having it off with Deirdre and Moira
(One blonde, t'other brunette,
Both sensational,)
Simultaneously.
So succulent and easy.

Succulent and easy,
The world is theirs and we built it.
Us,
The tweed-jacket-patched-at-the-elbows
Corduroy-trousers-with-turn-ups brigade,
Who fought the War
In the R.A.S.C. or the Ordinance Corps
"To build a better world".
And voted for Attlee
"To build a better world".
And worked through the fifties
On bread and dripping
"To build a better world".

"To build a better world".
And now the better world has been built,
Where Mr. Right
With his flowered ties
And new degrees
Tells us our methods are out of date,
And the better world's red tape
Has decided to sack us
For not possessing degrees,
For not being succulent
Or easy.

Not being succulent or easy —
Now that the better world is built —
In my last of seventy-five terms,
With a "Well-you-were-nearly-retirement-age-anyhow-
Must-make-way-for-younger-men-Jones"
And a slap on my shoulder
From our bluff, charcoal-suited headmaster,
On his way through us
To Wolverhampton Central Comprehensive,
Local Government and finally Parliament,
In my last term before enforced retirement
To a pocket-sized garden of beetroot
And non-prize-winning lettuce,
While I was planning my final Tempest
To culminate
A quarter-century of annual Shakespeares,
I'm summoned by my superceder
As Chairman of the English Department
With a "You-won't-mind-will-you-no-Shakespeare
Something-new-Jim-Wright's-dance-drama-
To-the-Sacre-de-Printemps-instead,"
And a "Kids-today-
Can't-relate-to-Shakespeare-
Sure-you-agree",
With a "Glad-of-what-help-you're-able-to-give"
From Mr. Right to me,
Not meaning one elocuted syllable.

We are such stuff
As dreams are made of.
This was my dream
In the chocolate and cream
School corridors.
Now they tell me I've dreamt enough,
And shut the doors.
We are the stuff of dreams,
And when the dreams acquire their shapes
The dreamer escapes . .
Pft! into thin air,
And like an insubstantial pageant fades,
Leaving nothing there.

My little life is rounded with a sleep.
This place
Is my entire space.
What is there for me to keep?
Only that sleep.

So with a "Jones-
He's-getting-a-bit-of-a-fusspot-isn't-he"
And a "Pity-he-has-to-go-
Bad-luck-this-degree-business",
With a "Maureen-hey-
You're-putting-on-weight-
Easy-on-chocolate-cream-
Till-after-the-production"
Fade into dribbles of verbs and multiplication tables
Fade into corduroy stained with beetroot
Fade into
Fade into
Fade into dreams of insubstantial
Fade into
Fade into
Fade
Out.

Poor old Jones
Knobbles on his bones
Patches on his elbows and his pocket full of groans

Poor old Jones
Knobbles on his bones
Patches on his elbows and his . . .

WHERE HAVE THEY GONE?

"Where have they gone?"

"I noticed some traces in that derelict building-site,
And what looked like footprints."

"Where did they go from here?"

"Look! Black smudges on the whitewashed wall
Of Incorporated Chemicals.
Could that be them? — Maybe they rested
Some minutes there in the sunshine."

"Where would they go from here?"

"There must have been two:
One of them, all on his own, moves ever so silently.
Once there are two or more,
They're always bounding and larking about
Whatever the danger."

"Oh where could they have gone?"

"We should really hope they are far away by now,
Chasing each other through buttercup meadows,
Then lying in feathery grass,
                    mouths crammed full of strawberries."

"I wonder where they went . . ."

"They're certainly well rid of us.
What jealousy, greed, suspicion . . .

Oh, we'll behave as we've always done,
Never having noticed
How, when they were here,
Light seemed a little more golden,
Flowers grew just a bit taller
With a more exuberant scent,
And as for the apple harvest . . .
Remember picking those cookers
                    that tasted like Cox's Orange Pippins.
Even the people, to their own amazement,
Could be seen relaxing their frowns and pouts and scowls."

THE MIRROR

Head cracks on the mirror.
Through, beyond the hard glass, dances the antiworld.

At one millisecond past midnight on Midsummer Eve
The glass becomes fluid.
World and antiworld swim through each other's brains.

Antiworld turns to an antechamber,
As we pass through to the hall beyond the mirror-room,
Gliding towards the kings.

But knocking your head on a mirror
Takes more than a millisecond.

The action cannot be timed.

For hundreds of Midsummer nights
The glass has kept its secret.

I AM A ROOM

I am a room
With grey birds pecking the windows,
And grubs on the floor,
Well-fed, brown and hairy.

But what are the grubs?
And what are the birds?

The grubs shrink into a corner,
Slump asleep.
Filaments of mist
Wind the chrysalids round them.

The grey birds peck-tap the windows,
Hunger with hammering eyes.
I am bombarded by nightmare vastness of wings.

But what are the grubs?
And what are the birds?

Will the grubs soar forth as orange and azure butterflies,
Shimmer and glitter through me
Like wind-tossed petals of sunlight,
Dodging for a few seconds the threat of the Luftwaffe beaks.

Or are the grubs
About to hatch as germ-sticky plague-sprouting flies?
Are the grim birds
Insectivore saviours
Purging my rot and infection?

One thing only I know: —
The moment a chrysalid bursts,
This window is programmed to open automatically.

THE VELVET TRAP

The roses, scent-suffused,
Man-trap your breath, anaesthetise.

The lady's peppermint lips
Ingest you with an octopus grip.

The melting chocolate sucks
You into sticky clutches.

Thousands of velvet pillows
Muffle your yells.

TILL THE PAIN SPINS . . .

Swallow that scarlet pain
Till the pain spins to a whipping-top.

Hands reach for a shriek
Which soars like Bird-of-Paradise.

Scars form on the breast
Ridges of vine-covered hills.

And the gushing blood
Flows into a pool of peace-leavened must.

HERE ON THIS HEAVING SURFACE

With sudden fog
Knifing our eyes and brain,
Black wings of panic
Pecking our ears,

While traps snap open,
Clutching our ankles,
And everywhere holes
Gape through earth's crust,

Our minds
No longer possessing streets and cities,
But only mountains and marshes'
Loose rock and squelching tussocks,

Here, on this heaving surface
Bombarded with lumps of molten cliff,
We have set our conference table.
Quick. We haven't much time in which to reach a decision.

NEVER A BIRD TO FLY

Never a bird to fly.
Never a fish to swim.
Never a beast to stalk the forests.
Only a dust-layered waste with thin
Films of grease, and a dim
Smoke-cloud hovering over the greed-flattened emptiness.

SMASH THE WHITE TOWERS

Vilanelle

Smash the white towers of pride, oh cleansing sea.
Shatter the engines, break the barrier walls.
With man wiped off its surface, earth is free.

Man's work mushrooms across the land. His fee
Increases daily for building marble halls.
Smash the white towers of pride, oh cleansing sea,

And as man feels within his grasp the key
To harness nature's power, let loose your squalls.
With man wiped off its surface, earth is free.

What matter if weak man squeal out, "Why me?
Why not my ancestors?" Laugh as he falls.
Smash the white towers of pride, oh cleansing sea.

Smash this attempt by man to reign, to be
God of this world. Bounce him like ping-pong balls.
With man wiped off its surface, earth is free

In the vast wildness of wave, cliff and tree.
So, with the mocking touch of waterfalls,
Smash the white towers of pride, oh cleansing sea.
With man wiped off its surface, earth is free.

LYING ON THE FLOOR WITH A SLIPPED DISC

On the floor
With the eyes becoming insect-sized,

On the floor
With the fluff and dust
Which accumulates under furniture,

On the floor
With a dead wasp's and dried
Twisted fly's
Miniature scrap-metal heap of bodies

Learn the lessons
Of human mortality:

How, with a flick
Of a twisted vertebra,
We become scrap-metal bodies,
For some large Presence to lift,
Slightly fastidiously pinching thumb and forefinger
On our dried wings,
And drop in the waste-bucket under a pile of old tea-leaves.

THE BLACK APE

Based on a true story

The black ape's principal food is fruit.
They are fond of attention and quite docile.
When they are pleased they expose their teeth
In a way very like a human smile.

They are known to have bred in captivity.
In the Javan forests they are found in groups.
Pongo was given a cage to himself,
Fitted with swings, and ropes with loops.

Every day the children would watch him swing
Or climb the spokes of his turning wheel.
They always peeled his bananas and pears,
Although he seemed to like the peel.

One Tuesday in August Pongo broke out,
Climbed over the roofs and played scapegrace.
He stole some fruit, but was still hungry,
And, teased by a child, he scratched its face.

A crowd gathered, with umbrellas and rakes,
And cornered him in a small bathroom.
Pongo grew savage; the police took charge;
And decided to administer chloroform.

They discovered the owner's name at last,
And a taxidermist stuffed the skin.
A zoologist, questioned on TV,
Affirmed that, in zoos, they are well locked in.

The black ape's principal food is fruit.
They are fond of attention and quite docile.
When they are pleased they expose their teeth
In a way very like a . . . human smile?

ON COMING ACROSS YARDS AND YARDS OF MAGNETIC SOUND TAPE STREWN OVER AN UPPER EAST SIDE STREET IN NEW YORK CITY

The streets of the city are strewn with magnetic tape.

All conversations, present and future,
Exist as physical entities.

Women are tying their lovers' remarks
Into ribbons for their hair.

Discussions to avert a strike by the garbage men
Are being dumped in the trash bins.

A Symposium on World Hunger
Is being fed to cattle instead of cellulose for rapid weight increase.

The streets of the city are strewn with magnetic tape.

People rushing to act
Trip over long strands of speeches calling for action,
And lie, tangled and strangled by thin brown streamers of words.

GARGOYLE

The only way to drown
In shallow water's keep nose down.

One way's to crawl so close
That the sand crabs nip your nose, —
Never mind your toes.

Or you can stand on your head;
But you make such a splash when you're dead.

Why not drown in your own armchair.
Stick your nose in a ladle of soup
And hold it there.

THE DEAD HERO AND THE LIVING FOLLOWERS

We have borne him wildly through heather and bent,
We have waved his death from the raven's crag.
His soul has unfurled its dragon flag
And jumped on its wind for the tournament.

Hunched in our hut that rattles with storm
For a peat-smoke evening of bacon-an'-eggs,
We uncurl the aches from our bog-trodden legs,
Poke flames - for his soul?

.   .   . or to keep ourselves warm?

FOR A DEATH IN THE SPANISH LANGUAGE

During September 1973 Pablo Neruda, greatest Spanish
poet of his generation, died while Chile's long tradition
of democracy was being destroyed by the tanks and guns
of soldiers.

Words in black hats,
Red sashes, white frilly shirts,
Zapateado away,
Heel-taps ratcheting rifle-shot over the boards
Kicked into drums of booming gunfire
Hollower, hollower, hollower.
Dust-cloud puffs out of machine-gun castanet rattles
Wisp through the empty barn,
Slightly shifting rat-corpses
                stretched mildew-like over the rubbish-heaps.

The dancers have fled from the bombs to the mountains.

Into the dust-battered void of the hall
Word-hags trundle the coffin,
Mumbling and scuffing the reverberating dust
Of exploded bodies, twisted fingernails,
Trails of decaying guts
And splatters of brain.
Beggar-words wheeze, shuffle up to the grimy catafalque.
Cracked gasps of broken-backed spittle,
Deformed dwarf question-marks,
Scrabble with knees, elbows, arthritic bird-claw fingers,
To salute thee, Pablo,
To salute that scarlet matador-lunge of language,
That fountain-head and mountain-spring
Now stuffed and choked with lumps of oily rag
Stinking of cordite.

FOR DAVID JONES

Hallowe'en 1974

David Jones was born on November 1st, All Saints'
Day, 1895. He died on October 28th, 1974. Just
before his death I had been filming him as the first
part of a documentary about his work. At the time
of his death I was in New York, and so heard of it
three days late, on Hallowe'en.

I met you as an image to be fastened on celluloid,
As words to be turned into pictures of mountains,
Sleeping warriors, chalices and machine-guns.
I'm going to have a spot of bother from the bureaucrats
Because you've died at this moment. So be it —
If I'm caught in the cross-fire of their memo-bullets,
Enfiladed by their telephone calls,
And no longer able to withdraw for an hour
To the behind-the-lines-French-farmhouse of your conversation.
Now, on this day of nervous trench silence,
While inside me the roar of the guns draws nearer,
I'm lifting my army-tin-mug of words to you
To praise your passing In Paradisum.
Tomorrow is the day of All Hallows.
I hope there'll be plenty in that company
To help you spend a pleasant eternity.
So . .
In Paradisum, David . .
In Paradisum . . .
In Paradisum . . . .

THE BIRTH OF AQUARIUS

An invented legend, but based on the original
Egyptian image of the Water-Carrier, bearing
the two rivers - the White and the Blue Nile.

for Chrys

The princess asleep

Crackling wafers of heat
Pressed from the pale ochre moon
On my bed reflecting the moon.
Bed like a bubble of glass in the sand.
Room and desert and bed
Heaved by me up through the air
Mirage-waving, quivering, cracking
Like rocks into lava . . .
Then the moistening hotness,
The soft glass blanket of darkness
Ripped off,
Exposing the room's glass bubble
To the brown, dusty, flattening heat of the moon
Sucking me up to its surface,
Scraping my skin transparent,
Scraping all space between horizons
Smooth with flat, beige drought,
The dark obliterated.

The princess dreams

The dark eye swells.
The last black gap in the moon
Swells to a point, a spike,
A pale beak of mirage,
Of silver waterfall,
And the pale blue kingfisher perched on my trembling feet,
Offers his boiling icicles –
"Quick.
Into your womb. Hide."
Then, grinning with lechery easy as water,
"Wait" he said, "for my white –
Wait for my silver brother" he said,
"Wait for the white kingfisher.
At dawn we shall greet you, and rape you together.
The white and the blue shall be one,
The twin beaks
Superimpose into one
Blue-silver waterfall of seed
Pouring your virgin blood on the sand
Black.
Your son
Will bear us, one on each shoulder,
As he ploughs his oatmeal desert,
Whose beige-coloured grit will grow softly black
With the gush of your blood from our beaks,
As we dive down his arms, transforming ourselves to rivers,
Till corn sprouts, giggling, between his toes,
And men chuck him moons of silver to trade for his grain,
While he lies, mounting his sister, begetting a rainbow of kings,
And calls you . . Egypt . . . . . "

The princess waits

For the heat pressed down into dawn
Like yeast into dough,
For the flat, beige cake of the moon,
Pressed in the round, oven bed, to rise.
For the dark gap winking.
For the glacier stream.
For the white frost of a beak,
Burning,
Pouring
The blue and silver icicles
Into one stabbing dive,
Vaster, brighter, faster than eagles . . .
Wait
For the fish to be caught, the minnow
To shrink and die
In a shaking-out, plummeting glint of feathers.

And after . . .

"The blue and the white beak came,
Stabbed from the moon through yeasty heat . . .

Out of this pain, a son,
Who'll water the world with the beaks
                    that flow from his shoulders.

But me . .
Me, lost in the pain,
In the beak that chewed and swallowed my womb.

Never for me shall be love, but only bleeding."

THE POET'S BALANCE: TWO SESTINAS

for Peter

1. THE POET'S NIGHTMARE

Written after a conversation with a publisher friend. We were
discussing our attitudes to rock-climbing. He had been
climbing solo recently and admitted that he needed to prove
himself by frequently risking death. I said that I no longer did
any very dangerous climbs. He said 'Of course not. I can see
from your poetry that you find all the risks you need in
personal relationships.'

Grope forward. Hands stretching for holds. Void. Darkness.
Emptiness. Blank. Stretch further. Heaving nightmare
Of an infinite nothing-vista. Struggle
Through marshland void to reach a void of ridges,
Gullies and lava-flow. What chance survival?
Impossible to see hands before face.

Somewhere behind this darkness, a dark face
Composed of nothing more than well-warmed darkness
Welcomes me to a void, but built.— Survival
From cold with snow-block shelters? — In this nightmare
The nightmare shapes itself to a landscape. Ridges
And gullies form as aids to this vague struggle.

Out of the vagueness, void. But through the struggle
Against the void, directly up the face
Of the sheer void, we can traverse to ridges
Still formed from void, from non-finger-hold darkness,
But, by a tiny fraction, more solid nightmare
Than total void. Now, might there be survival?

So bang fingers against the frost. Survival? —
Nail-scratching clutch and slither. Balance. Struggle
From finger-hold to hold. Boot-edge scrapes face
Of sheerness. All around a swirling nightmare
Of mist, snow-scurrying. But the blank darkness
Turns to grey cloud, horizons, lines of ridges.

Up, struggle up, edge leftwards to the ridge's
Relative relaxation. Now, survival
In the ice-wind. But up. Up from the darkness.
Now we can walk; use legs; step. Now this struggle
Yields some results. Now we can see a face
Of a companion also climbing nightmare.

No longer void now, the elusive nightmare
Becomes rock-hard, sharp as the granite ridge's
Jagged hand-holds. Hard and smooth as the face.
But now there's solid chance of our survival.
There is a solid ridge up which we struggle.
Might there be sunrise? An end to this darkness?

So we confront each darkness, risk its nightmares,
Struggle through each night's void-land to its ridges,
Chalking up each survival on our marked face.

2. THE POET'S SENSUALITY

Lounge on the beach. Drinks. Pot. The living's easy.
Fridge and dish-washer. Doorman for the complex
Of service apartments. Nothing here is painful.
Winter is warm. You can indulge your senses
In sun and booze and sex. Plenty of loving!
And plenty of money without much need to work.

Result:— this poetry, with nothing worked
Over, no shape, no drive. It's all too easy.
Maybe there has to be restraint, if loving's
To flourish. "Oh, you people are so complex."
No. Sensuality does not mean senses
To be indulged at whim. To sense is painful.

Breathe in. Smell air. Each breath we draw is painful
On mountain-tops. But what a cleansing. Work
At sensitising each of our weak senses.
Tuning our instrument. No action's easy.
But by control of each of our most complex
Activities we can control our loving,

And tune that too, till we exist by loving
Each breath of air, each insect's flight, each painful
Movement of muscle, and learn and grow and work
Everything through us, till our tangled, complex
And warring wants and feelings flow in easy
Rhythms which harmonise all of our senses.

Now, watch, sniff, touch, taste, listen. Now our senses
Twang with the colours, smells and sounds. We, loving
Each moment of the day, will find it easy
To draw into our joy movements once painful
To our desensitised bodies. Our work
And pain can grow together as one complex.

The beetle stirs. Smell pines. Lace boots. A complex
Pattern of action dances through our senses,
Forming inside our minds, turning to work
Deep in us - shaped words, coloured, sensual, loving
And disciplined. This rock feels hard and painful.
But climbing is not climbing if too easy.

Shrinking is easy. To grow involves a complex
And painful struggle to discipline our senses
Into such loving that we relax by work.